IN A PIG'S EYE

IN A PIG'S EYE

by

Robert Siegel

A University of Central Florida Book

UNIVERSITY PRESSES OF FLORIDA
FAMU/FAU/FIU/FSU/UCF/UF/UNF/USF/UWF
Orlando

University of Central Florida
Contemporary Poetry Series

Other works in the series:

Van K. Brock: *The Hard Essential Landscape*
Malcolm Glass: *Bone Love*
Susan Hartman: *Dumb Show*
David Posner: *The Sandpipers*
Edmund Skellings: *Heart Attacks*
Edmund Skellings: *Face Value*

University Presses of Florida, the agency of the State of Florida's
university system for publication of scholarly and creative works,
operates under policies adopted by the Board of Regents. Its offices
are located at 15 Northwest 15th Street, Gainesville, Florida 32603.

Library of Congress Cataloging in Publication Data

Siegel, Robert, 1939–
In a pig's eye.

(Contemporary poetry series) (A University of Central
Florida book)
 I. Title. II. Series: Contemporary poetry series (Or-
lando, Fla.)
PS3569.I38215   811´.54   80-13313
ISBN 0-8130-0679-1

Acknowledgments

The author is grateful to the following publications for assignment of copyrights and permission to reprint the poems that originally appeared in their pages: *America:* "Mayflies: The Hatch" (formerly "The Hatch at Thetford Pond"; reprinted by permission of America Press, Inc., 106 West 56th St., New York, NY 10019, © 1980—all rights reserved); *Beloit Poetry Journal:* "Sow's Ear"; *Colorado Quarterly:* "Draining a Mosquito Swamp"; *Cream City Review:* "The Moonseed," "The White Sow of Marengo"; *The Humanist:* "Sheep at Nightfall" (formerly "Sheep"); *Kodon:* "Shopping Together"; *The Midwest Quarterly:* "Simple Simon" (formerly "Spastic"); *New England Review:* "Now They Stand Still," "Submariner"; *New York Quarterly:* "Sow Moon"; *Poetry:* "A Lady Who Lov'd a Swine," "Bull," "Hog Heaven," "Knave of Hearts," "Them," copyright © 1974, 1977 by the Modern Poetry Association; *Prairie Schooner:* "Barney Bodkin," "Christmas Eve," "Hans and His Wife," "In a Pig's Eye" (formerly "To Market, To Market"; reprinted under that title in *Best Poems of 1976*), "Like Butter," "Mound," "Peonies," "Pomfret Apples," "Sumac," "Widower," copyright by the University of Nebraska Press.

The author is grateful to the Yaddo Corporation for two residencies during which he worked on many of the poems, and especially to Polly Hanson for her encouragement then and afterwards. He wishes to thank Dartmouth College, the University of Wisconsin, and the Ingram Merrill Foundation for grants providing substantial periods of time to work on the collection.

He expresses special gratitude to Roland Browne for his thoughtful and inspired editorial help; to Richard S. Grove, Laurence Lieberman, and Joseph Parisi for their suggestions for the manuscript; to Charles Young for his cover design; to the staff of University Presses of Florida for their professional attention to the publication of his book; and, last, to his wife Ann for help in arranging the poems and for her sure insight in an endless number of critical deliberations.

Contents

To Ann

1

I saw my true love
In a pig's eye.

Sow Moon

Sow with silver jowl
low to the horizon, rooting the hills,
what is it you look for where trees huddle
about the new smells?

You roll over the earth,
back glistening with a sweat of stars.
Deep in the swamp the peepers
shrill and blink their eyes.

Mud mother, teat and loin
hairy with forests,
the dogwood, the thorn
wild on your snout,

Great Flowering Swine
browsing the hills,
nosing the green troughs
with summer's silken ear,

out of the sweet husks
of Missouri spring you come
stirring the mast
of my naked heart.

Vast belly, glimmering
with a million nipples,
on whom the earth turns
and feeds all night.

What Does the Pig Think of the Dawn?

> *What does the pig think of the dawn?*
> *They do not sing but hold it up*
> *with their huge rosy bodies,*
> *with their hard little hooves.*
>
> —Neruda

Yes, the pigs hold it up,
they stand like clouds,
banks of roses,
they rise out of glittering mud
squeezing air from their snouts
like warring pipers,
as the sun burns against their bristles,
making forest fires along their spines.

They lounge and scruff,
pushing rings through the dirt,
bump and back off like blimps,
but stand still when the boar shifts his shadow,
ears wagging like awnings,

when he of the thick neck,
whose eyes are steady and small,
red and small as embers,
grunts and scratches himself against a post,

then moves to the corn,
deliberate as a storm front,
and bites it, tossing the cob in the air,

kernels flying from the curved trench of his mouth,
as if to say, *See where I toss it?*
Is there one who would go after it now?
watching the sows — *Is there one?*

The others, in a circle, pretend not to watch,
but they are watching,
tails curled tight. None eats.
He in that wide circle feels the sun,
feels himself the cloud floating before it.

He moves back to his pen,
each leg propping his bulk,
easing like the Hindenburg to its berth.
All hold their breath.
There in the shadow he sprawls as dust
rises like a red dream over him.

The young ones begin
here and there to chew a cob.
The squeals and tentative grunts grow louder.
A few barge and bully each other.
Meanwhile, a bluebottle buzzes over the eye,
oysterish, half-open,
fixed in his darkness like the North Star.

Ego

has thrust his nose under every board,
smelt out every wild carrot and white grub,
stucco'd the dirt with his tracks from side
to side, rubbed smooth the corner
posts, left his pink, red-bristled hide
on every barb of five strands of wire;

chews the bark from the one scrub pine
that pitches a ghost of shade at noon,
bangs incessantly the metal trough-lid
at off-hours, chuffs down the white meal,
raising a cloud around his ears, and cleans
each cob with the nicety of a Pharisee,

tooth for tooth, squeezing contentedly
his small bagpipe voice as he mashes
corn with a slobbery leer and leaves
turds like cannonballs across a battlefield.
Meanwhile his little pink eye is
periscoped on the main chance—

the gate ajar, the slipped board,
the stray ducky that flusters through the wire—
saliva hanging from his mouth like a crown jewel.
His jowls shake with mirth under the smile
that made a killing on the market, won the fifth caucus,
took the city against all odds.

No wonder we shake at the thought
of his getting out, electrify the wire.
(At night we hear him thump his dreams
on the corrugated tin hut and shudder,
the single naked bulb in there burning
through our sleep like his eye!),

take special dietary precautions against
his perpetual rut, except that March day
we drag the yearling sow to him
through mud up to her hocks. From that handseling
comes the fat litter—the white one for the Fair,
the spotted black to be slaughtered in November.

We don't show him to the neighbors, though in June,
framed by clover and bees stringing out the sun, he is
quite grand, an enormous blimp supporting
intelligent waggish ears, regally lidded eyes and
a pink, glistening snout
ready to shove up the privates of the world.

Sow's Ear

> *Here comes a lusty Wooer,*
> *My a Dildin my a Daldin,*
> *Here comes a lusty Wooer,*
> *Lilly bright and shine, A.*

Fifty sows dozing in the hard-packed yard,
fifty sows, all sizes, from purple majesty
to pink ninny,
fifty, sluttish, given to untidy houses,
the open robe of morning, flea in the ear,
snorting, swilling the hay-strewn water;
some indifferent as the Sierra Madre
steaming over deserts, features lost
in foothills and ridges of fat;
others petulant, bristling,
practicing the small clean bite.

The lean young boar, thick-necked,
walks a plank from the truckbed,
razor-backed, tufted, tusks rounded to ball-bearings,
lord of the mountains, the hills of flesh,
the little valleys spread before him.

He is small, but the muscles of his neck
can break a hound, or a man's leg.

First one, sullen, whitish-purple in the heat,
stands off, pegs the dirt — mean hussy —
grunts, *Come show me, Bastard!*
Grunts, and grunts again.

Though he doesn't turn toward her, he sees her.
Still, he waits for her waddling run,
her little yellow teeth
bared for the swipe at his haunch,
swivels and knocks her off balance —
blood pudding, sack of fat!
Terror curdling from her throat, she
telegraphs herself to a far corner,
peg peg peg peg peg.

The second, caught off-guard,
lies where she falls, croaking.

But the third,
mother of clouds and mountains,
400 pounds of mauve-and-pink repose,
feels their cries stoke a fire in her bowels,
a vein of lava creep from marble hams,
through vesuvial lungs,
to the flexing crab of her brain.
Uncertainly, on one leg, then two,
she jacks herself from the primal pool
where gnats nidder and dance.
Mud swings crusted on her teats,
falls in patches from her belly:

What are these that tickle the brain?
Love's tiny cries? The yammering mouths?
Squeals that hang like sausages?
No, not those tender attentions.

Dimly, she remembers something
unlocked from her, a tremor, a quake,

an eruption,
when once she opened and
free of her hulk
the delicate she of a dream
danced like rain on a corrugated roof,
pooled in cool wallows,
sprouted under tender thistle,
rolled in goldenrod and clover,
frisked with cat and suckling.

Turning toward him like a locomotive
on its turntable, the steam
of her memories creasing all her jowls
to one truculent smile, she charges:

Oh to be the blue fly, the bee, golden,
jigging above the ticklish purple!
                    BANG
Aye, this is the rub,
the tickle of love! she snorts, enamored.
                    BANG
O honey bee! Sweetling,
hungry for my attentions!

Again she turns where the boar, dizzy
and sore in the neck, stands baffled.
Having assaulted with his head the Himalayas,
having not gotten over the foothills,
he staggers in disbelief
as Everest trundles toward him.

This is the one! Husband! she croons,
full and resonant as a bullfrog,
Sweet chop, my porker, my honey cob!

O what a squall of pipers,
what a regiment of bloodcurdling love,
dooms over the highlands of her corpus
resounding from glen and hillside
as she advances on him in a corner,
stale and snuffed as Macbeth,
head slung low, as all the world marches on him,
to meet the fate, perilous, magnificent,
of fathering five-hundred friskers.

In a Pig's Eye

> *Hickamore, Hackamore,*
> *Why do you sigh?*
> *I saw my true love*
> *In a pig's eye.*

She couldn't (or could she?)
live with the three chins,
the mouth that took the world
to its plush accordion,
Dutch seas of gravy, a cigar
angling, the *Titanic*'s last stack
above its foundering hulk.

His hands over the omelet were
immaculate, the nails' white
quarter moons dancing, while one
big opal seemed to feast an eye
on her through coffee, mints,
and velvet gastronomic sigh.
(She resolved she couldn't!)

Pushing the table back, he was
Atlas shrugging off the world,
Napoleon rolling it toward the stars —
so complete his every gesture.
How odd, she laughed, all this!
The man was obscene, selfish.
Smiling, his wet lips pursed

to a primrose. Yet, squeezing into
cabs, puffing up red-carpeted stairs,
he courted her—she let herself
be courted—those two jowls hemispheres
into which all fell left
or right. A diamond big as a parfait
he said, his red tongue winking.

Rice salted down the two of them
in the dark car that glided home
to the earthquake of his bed,
where for a moment sweet terror
stalked her, rabbit in a white field.
Then the sun fell on her and the moon and, oh,
she danced above the seas a light rain,
and, tasted, drunk, folded to the earth,
slept quiet as his rib again.

A Lady Who Lov'd a Swine

I'll build thee a silver stye,
  Honey, quoth she,
And in it thou shall lye:
  Hoogh, quoth he.

It was those little teeth she loved most
showing at breakfast, the road-mapped
eyes over the shaking O of coffee,
the snuffling and snorting behind the paper,

as if his anger built a factory
behind a paper scaffold, a plant
to electrify her kitchen, made a place
of scorched toast, a Red Sea of counters

drained flat when he left. The ticking
fly-leg in the clock stamped each second.
She'd sit in the elastic mouth
of the armchair, rubbing a purple bruise

he'd given her last night — corsage
aching with color, drunkard's lovebite —
while the air waltzed with dust
and pain roosted in her nest of hair.

The brisk *chnnk* of mail in the box
would send her to the door, opening which
she'd let in the sun in its pert
gossipy way to enquire,

How could she stand living with the brute?
Didn't her face need re-upholstering?
She hugged the insult back to bed
like a hotwater bottle.

In the March afternoon she'd try to dig
up bird cries buried in the yard,
something muffled the sun might coax loose,
all the while listening for his shadow

and booming demand for a drink, his beery cheek
sanding her neck as he squashed her to him
tilting toward the icebox and boozy dreams
of swilling all night with the squealing girls.

And she would droop down willingly and listen to the ice
ring music, ring money, under a porcine stare
puerile and crafty — *Dearest, dearest piggy*
of her heart, rooting hot, stamping at the rails,
rummaging the husks of her endless love!

Hog Heaven

for NA and KP

In some dim sense he sees
it is already here,
the field of delicate corn, the glittering
wallow where each rolls free
of the hill of flesh, of the jawless appetite
that inhales a world of garbage and shrieks *More*
(as if the skin didn't have a decent limit) —
that tries to thrust himself upon himself
until all flesh balloons to one vast Pig
on which he is the smile, satisfied.

Dozing on the warm cement he dreams
that the sun, puzzled, pauses in the heavens,
that *First one at the trough for swill*
and *Furthest from the draft at night*
are not enough,
that the sun-warmed fly, who now forgets to bite,
buzzes another tongue, and the lifting wind
sneaks glittering through the goldenrod
to whisper something else into his ear
before the whistle blows, *It's time for slops.*

Like straw such dreams trouble the water's surface —
the pig's persistent business of stuffing, rutting
and grunting to his fellows his narrow will —
until the box pulls up and the ham-faced farmer,
with hands like shovels and two sly-footed dogs,

directs him into terror's empty room
over an engine mumbling and shaking like a fly.
Too late — he cannot think for the squealing mob,
hunger, cold, and dust thick in his snout.

But after three days without water,
sensing the golden sacrifice of bacon,
the roast's crackling holocaust,
he rises, hilarious as helium
and, wingéd above the anonymous pen,
a winter gaiety glazing his eye,
a seraphic humor slimming his jowl,
foresees and forgives all:
the rotating jaws, the dreamless fat and muscle,
the bland pink hands which lift the plate for more.

The White Sow of Marengo

This little pig stayed home.

Cloud of flesh
you pin the field down
so it won't rise, rip out the seam of trees
and flap over the swamps to Chicago.

You turn the light to milk
and happily lie
dozing toward China, lending the earth
the gross momentum of your bulk.

As I pass, an incurious eye
follows my head above the fence,
and five chins smile at one
who

unlike you and the sun
drags a flickering shadow over the earth.

2

*The whole creation groaneth
and travaileth . . . together.*

Them

> *There are men in the village of Erith*
> *Whom nobody seeth or heareth.*
> *And there looms on the marge*
> *Of the river, a barge*
> *That nobody roweth or steereth.*

On the shore of the river where you picnic,
a part of the day is missing
that was there in your bright predictions,
a blank like the sand in your sandwich

that can't be gotten rid of, though you try
shifting your seat. At the office
the paper crawling under your pencil
is significantly silent about them.

In class when someone writes on the blackboard,
these leave a slight chalky aura
that fades when the bell rings. You wonder
what it was they were going to make clear.

At home they play cribbage in the parlor,
silently advancing the pegs
while you in the kitchen have forgotten
the salami and rye you came out for.

Walking out, you sense them already
before you around the corner,
find their fingerprints on the windows,
their breath rising over the shingles.

At last, though you've no wish to see them,
you find you cannot live without them,
for, foul-breathed, dark with loose threads,
or radiant, eaten by light,

one will, one day, lift a hand
and the map on his hand will match yours.

Knave of Hearts

Maybe he comes in the window,
maybe lies under the bed
with an old slipper collecting thoughts
in great balls that creep at a draft.
But at night I

sitting in a moon of lamplight hear
you going to bed, the whisper of your dress,
the bed's complaining chuckle. Still my book
clasps me by the middle,
opening itself page by page.

Yet there it is, the silk of your breathing,
his voice in the wall like electricity.
The doorknob flashes and winks, my hand lifts
toward it, but sunk in words, in the chair,
I cannot escape the lamp's circle.

Under the sheets I would find you sleeping,
your peach nightie bunched up, your breasts
perfuming a foreign market
and every clue of him gone as he hovered
in a circle around the bed, waving ghostly fingers.

As he did the night I chased him
into the blue fixtures of the bathroom,
hoping the hard, buzzing light would hold him,
catch his reflection in the mirror, unshaven,
sinking toward the razor—

only to hear the airshaft open,
a long rising sigh,
and the last troubled stars
dancing in the heat of his lust.

Bull

Flies crawling the map of his ear
     do not bother him.
His eye has the long look of history.
     When he blinks
the tizzy settles somewhere else.

On cold mornings he snorts twin
     blue mushrooms, his hide
bearing a starwork of frost
     as if he sprung whole from the sleep
of Babylonian astronomers.

His hoof divides the dust.
     It is precisely out of this scrape
came his appetite for geometry —
     to eat the earth piece by piece.
Then wonder put a hook in his nose

and he lay among milk-white cows
     who sang upon harps of sunlight
swaying in the grasses
     until his heart ran with pity,
gored by a purple wound.

Now with a brass ring for his law
     he stands in a lake of shade
watching us, inconstant white things
     among goldenrod, purple thistle,
alert for the bloody insult — still,

only half a mind to malice,
  dreaming among his blue flowers:
ready to kick the world to static,
  if need be, if need be, but listening,
as the earth builds and the pollen blows,
  to the small crazy song of the bee.

Widower

> *Little Dicky Dilver*
> *Had a wife of silver;*
> *He took a stick and broke her back*
> *And sold her to the miller.*
>
> *(The wife of silver in this*
> *old riddle is a stalk of rye.)*

Again, again, I mow your yellow hair.
The dead elm watches over us like your mother
and the scythe keeps polishing its blind smile.
Clouds of pollen settle on the river

where the cow got stuck last week, eyes bugging.
We pulled her from the mud, green as a frog,
and felt the earth shudder where you lie
buried, the orchards and streams of your body

coiling under the wood, leaking at the springs —
like the cow, helpless, reptilian.
At night a phosphorus moon swims down the sky,
lonely, unpricked by the stars. I wake,

my body marble in the leaning light.
At dawn I rise, skim the moon's shadow
from a pan of milk, my shirt prickly with chaff,
and strap the horse to the fields

where you are already waving, gold upon gold.
I strip and sweat over the scythe,
seeking you, seeking you,
grinding my crooked knife against a stone.

Sheep at Nightfall

They are foam collecting
    on the shore of the field.
Backs yellow with dust
    they lean against the gate,
now one, now another, lifting a voice
    vibrating and torn as the Irish.

They are richly dressed, each wigged
    like a British justice. Yet
they move together like slaves
    bent under Pharaoh,
to be folded into the dark
    eating every green thing
and complaining at the dust of their daily bread.

If March shows the icy
    back of his robe,
they will go no further.
    Eyes thick with rheum
they feel death's finger shake the ground:
    Thousands in one night
rot where they fall like patches of late snow.

Still the old ram carries his head
    like the treasure of Persia,
uttering a melodious question,
    knowing he will be answered
when the sun comes striding
    from the oratorio of the hills
touching his fleece with gold.

You Wore the Heat and Light of Wheatfields

You wore the heat and light of wheatfields
like Tutankhamen his gold,
embalmed each afternoon in sweat.
Rocking home
on the metal-cleated John Deere,
you felt it cool under your arms,
giving off a satisfying myrrh.

You wore a handkerchief against the dust
that climbed about you in clouds
and silted-in the wrinkles round your eyes.
Each night you turned out a small Eden
from your cuffs and left the Nile delta in the tub.

At twilight, in a clean shirt
you drank what air sifted through the screen.
The old Norge sputtered over its secret, a melon
whose red heart you split for us to gorge,
lining up seeds like Noah's animals.

Yet, chiefly, I recall you at noon,
straining to finish the harvest:
The whole parched, itching world rose up
glittering like frankincense,
as you sneezed, swore, jammed the tractor into first,
and laid it behind you mile by gold square mile.

Muskie

Eyes hoarding dull gold he lurks
at the bottom
holding the lake steady
in water the color of bock beer.
He has aged for decades —
in season, out of season.

Above him motors unzip the sky all day
and zip it up again
as he lies under layers of water
turning the drowsy
silk of his fins, watching shapes
panic across his ceiling.

Light fades. The wind drops.
Shapes grow clearer
on the surface, except for a wavering
ghost of birches, the quick cipher
of waterbugs. A yellow lamp
gleams and dissolves.

Then, from under the dark
fallen tree he shoots
on a straight tack, seizing
the sputtering plug, diving
against the light,
shaking the first stars from his tail.

Hauled-in, black and silver,
blood mapping his throat,
chewing the air of a pitiless altitude,
he beats a tattoo
on the aluminum hull, listening
to the deep waters
grow still
more silver in a moon that climbs
finless, among the stars.

Water Snake

The color of mud, the color of water
sliding beneath him,
he slips from the branch with an obscene ease,
plops, and hurries God knows where.

The branch rises slightly in the air:
Something on the mind has gone
under. Birds chirp, boys whistle
as the last stones sink after him.

Soon, their pale bellies flash
in his secret places —
the mud against which he was invisible,
the tree he tied himself to.

They shout, they dive,
break sticks against the willow.
They splash each other, washing off
the pensiveness of killers.

Later, when their voices die away
the water reveals a yellow S
drifting downstream,
purple sac bulging from its side.

A breeze crawls over the water
toward this armless, legless mouth,
thin as a nightmare
rocking toward the shallows of first sleep.

Jack Be Nimble

In Breughel's Icarus, *for instance,*
how everything turns away
Quite leisurely from the disaster . . .
— W. H. Auden

No, it wasn't like that at all. They were
with him every millisecond,
from the take-off, as the earth dropped away,
through the ascent, fake flame-out, and hover,
to the reverse twist when the reflected sun
flashed in their eyes aching to take in
this and all his other sleights-of-stick.

No, you can't say they didn't feel
every milligram of pressure on the throttle
as his helmet spun around and round
and he arrowed toward the unbreakable
line of the horizon.

As one man, they gasped
when his piece of glittering sky
(describing a perfect corkscrew, later
played over a thousand waiting stations)
barely touched the water,
raising a long geyser of spume,
consistently diminishing
as he came apart
to fire, water, air, nothing at all —

and all together watching breathed out, *Ah!*

Proboscis Monkey

We stop by the ape with a human nose,
an exclamation point between his eyes
suggesting purpose and a capacity for error.

While other apes swing or shuffle in a circle,
he hunkers down within his private space.
His nose gives him a beginning and an end.

Lurking in a back room of our skulls
like a melancholy prince, he seems
about to break out in soliloquy —

thinks better of it, snuffs like a selectman,
gazes at his hairless offspring,
who stares back with the same large doubtful nose.

We move on, amused by such a mirror,
tossing peanuts, wisecracking to each other,
glad that someone's gone to the expense

of caging up the far ends of the earth
that we might study our captivity,
who have the free horizon but cannot grasp it.

Submariner

She lost him to the dull light
fanning the pier where the submarine
slept on lean haunches. In months to come
the land heaved to the slow
tide of battle, news that
washed across the front pages.

Censored, his letters brought
accounts of boredom, ice cream,
hints of Bombay, Madagascar.
She stuck pins in a map, following
imaginary voyages until some fact
unstuck them all,
teasing her again across the endless
harp of longitudes.

At night his underwater shadow
slid through her dreams
into seas jewelled with disaster.
Pillows nuzzling her breast,
in thunder and lightning she felt
a mortal tremor of ships;
her windows sang like angels
to white ghosts of war.

Bearded, sea-changed,
he returned,
lifting her like the globe
lovingly this way and that,

his duffel spilling
her letters and an ocean's
weight of tears.

Still, the undersea shadow
cruised her dream, its eye
a work of winking light and pearls.
The faint hum and turbulence
of steel shapes passed,
fading to a gull's derisive cry
where waves scribbled
and erased a shore.
Then stiff with sleep he'd rise
and take her in arms
blue from the ocean.

The dreams passed.
At last, only her letters recalled
secretly to themselves
her underwater fear,
the long tapestry of nights
by which she shuttled him home
crabwise from the sea,
beggar with a star pinned to his shoulder.

Now They Stand Still

Horses grazing by the river
stamp and raise their heads,
proud in the mirror of each other's gaze,
forelocks shy as grass.

Meanwhile the river
slides with their ghosts to the sea,
sheet after sheet, each brighter than the last,
as the sky opens a vein of pure copper.

On the near side
uncertain with crickets,
smells of grass tangle in my nose,
a chill climbs from the shallows
up the hairs of my arm,
and the small torpedo of the frog
hits the water.

Still, while mist rises,
quietly attentive,
and places damp hands on my forehead,
I would dig my heel in to leave
a sharp imprint,
I would say something, a word
fraying at the edges like a star.

Barney Bodkin

Barney Bodkin broke his nose,
Without feet we can't have toes;
Crazy folks are always mad,
Want of money makes me sad.

for Sabina, in a state
ward for the senile

"It's Barney Bodkin holds us in,
I've often thought. He looks so queer
with his nose like a great eggplant,
the stethoscope hooked to each ear,

as if he's trying to figure where
that last bit of life is raising hell
on its little drum. In this hospital
I've noticed, to be ill is to be well:

For those who lift their chins over
the rail and pule and cry
for their teeth, are let down
by a white hand — sometimes tied

and spoonfed a sugary poison.
Ach! I got wise the first week,
saw the lively wheeled to the inner ward,
the still ones washed out with the sheets.

Now from this crib I watch herself
who brings me food on a steel plate
to see if she has the password: her eyes
go blank like the *Cream o' Wheat.*

Then Barney comes thumping and squeezing
and listening, trying to catch the little seed
that tickles in one ear and out the other,
running loose among his patients, who need

quiet he says — the quiet he carries
boxed in his cabbagey hand, nodding
like a tomato plant, listening
to where the earth way down is dead.

Oh, I pretend to be asleep or too dim
to notice his fingers brush over me, nor yet
his cold root pinching my arm,
his breath about my head like African violets.

I am better than he thinks: my sheets are clean,
mornings I count my toes twice over,
checking out both eyes, and know
they'll get the message to me wherever.

And some blue-bulbed night
after Bodkin has scraped past here
with that tiffley long vegetable breath of his,
I will inch over the bars,

slip out of this disguise they put me in,
and squeeze through that window
toward the river
where the others are holding up the stars."

Mayflies: The Hatch

for KS

Still they rise
like stars from the void,
light gone out or not yet kindled.
Each lies flat the pulse of an instant,
then stirs, a small vibrating rose.

At this moment the trout
comes or does not come,
sudden as a trumpet,
blowing a halo of bubbles.

It is no wonder,
lopsided with panic,
each wobbles into flight,
laboring in circles
just above the water.

(Even now a rainbow
may leap after,
rush it back to the deep
like a guilty kindness.)

Then,
straight up,
one after another,
each writes a secret name in the air,
ascending a moth-white sky
to vanish in solid cover.

Simple Simon

Now he wags his head, now beats the floor,
out of time with all the dignity,
pomp, and music in this service of our Lord,
this tread and pause of elders steady as trees.
Constrained inside his head all leaps and pushes
to a blur of light, to a hugger-mugger joy,
as if a wind would take each hand and rush
him birdlike to the altar with a cry.

We see his ungainly shadow, not
what his soul by its sharp hunger proves —
that we are fickle with our faculties
and by our spastic wills evade our love —
unlike this simple child whose spirit easily
outstrips where angels groan and dare not.

Christmas Eve

While cattle stupidly stare
over straw damp from their breathing
and the horse lazily stirs
over his trough, and the lantern
licks at shadows in corners,

in the woods the wild ones gather,
the rabbit twitching with care,
sooty shrew, and imperial mole
with the hands of a lost politician,
to shine in the branch-broken light

of a moon which in mid-career
lights up a church of snow.
Now one paw after another
about the bones of weeds
in a soft worrying circle

the helpless ones dance out their fear,
watching the glittering air
where he shines in the eyes of the others
naked, with nothing to wear.
Long before he comes to the stable

to the shrew's moving smudge on the snow
to the mole's ineffectual gesture
to the soft hide of the hare
he comes, warming each creature
naked in the fangs of the year.

Hans and His Wife

Moving in a ghost of starch, she'd brood above
her garden like a cloud soiled with rain,
perspiration steaming her glasses. Through them,
fuzzy green cabbages rose up like dwarves
from an underground kitchen in which she was
Dutch Cleanser girl. She'd bend and grunt,
twisting off their heads, filling her apron with
eyeless faces, carrot noses, blood-red beets
dribbling down Chinese beards.

Afternoons, shaded by the apple tree,
she'd fall asleep over white potatoes
skinless and cool in a bucket, sharing
her faint smell of starch — a knife at rest
half-way around a spud. Breathless, sweating,
we'd creep along behind the asparagus
and listen to her snore in German:
Ach . . . Ach . . . followed by a long thin whistle.

Rattling flowerpots indoors, Herr Spratt
showed his nose only at twilight, a kind of weasel,
tinkering and swearing aloud in dark spaces
behind the bird-limed trellis and flaking clapboards.
Herr Spratt vill fix it! she'd say of any
thing our folks brought to her, though we never
saw him do it. Tight gray jacket buttoned
up to his goiter, his polished glasses winked
with a steely love of engines and a honed
dislike of children — who knew all along

he worked fanatically on a secret V-2 rocket,
chuckling over it like screws loose in a box.

At six their garden filled with a vague absence
as ghosts of cabbages steamed up their kitchen windows.
Crouched, we'd listen to the sputtering confession
of the chops, the screaming kettle, the precise
clink and clank of torture going on for hours,
as knives and forks marched by in perfect order
across their plates and followed us to bed
under a damp and watery green moon.

Next morning when we woke, night clinging to us,
already she'd be out under a white sky,
calmly, as if she hadn't blood on her hands,
hoisting carrots up by the hair,
digging potatoes up from their blind sleep,
shaking the pale sun from her dirty apron.

Pomfret Apples

There was an old wife did eat an apple.

Through the sweet fumes of orchards,
the sun, round and red,
sinks as a toothless old woman
walking up to us smiles
like an apple bitten into.

Light as cornleaves her hands
slowly spell out our money
under the deepening orange
glow of pumpkins. The air
sizzles faintly with cider,
ripens with things put up,
while wrinkled heads of squash
dream the descending winter.

Apples safe in our trunk,
our tires number the driveway
stones, slip onto asphalt,
the tailpipe singing
blue clouds of exhaust to the night
as we follow a chain of red eyes
winking over the hills.

Back in the apple barn
the dog yawns once in the musk
of sleep stealing over him.
A cat leads eight shadows to bed.

The farmer and his wife
sink into sheets of snow.

Anemic with moonlight our car
hungers for a sign of home,
while in back our children stir
dreaming fitfully toward the rest
deep and untroubled of those
whose cellar sweetens with apples.

3

This reach beyond this death, this act of love
In which all creatures share, and thereby live.
—Roethke

Triptych

1. Oil Spill

You are in the small gray light
that wakes from the east, the shore
that outlines my day. Empty
sky is your medium. You promise

nothing to me who beach
like a ruptured supertanker
glutting the shore with oil,
slick gull, dying of surfeit.

I wade out, coated
with unctuous night.
Stones cut my feet—
my tongue crusted with sand.

Immerse me again, wash clean
the broken feather of my will.
Dry me with your wind,
massage my sluggish heart.

Then drop me from the bluff
into sharpening light,
where for hours I may climb
the thermal updraft of your breathing.

2. Sumac

Is this field your face pressed to the sky
as to the dull window of a train station?
The yellow grasses walk every which way,
lean together, bright in the rain.

No identifiable eyes, mouth, nose,
just a patient, sodden skin
lacerated by the yellow tractor whose dull blade,
smeared with red clay, is cocked at an angle

for its Sunday sleep. The dog runs
through cockleburs, shakes himself.
I press down and down the patient grass
that smells like wet clothes.

Nothing is doing in this rain.
Even the horizon is legendary
through watery smoke. But in a patch
of still green grass, a red sumac

claws open my heart. Small and constant,
the gray world suffers this beauty,
as when your skin, dissolving under lead in a riot
of blood, touched everything off like tinder.

3. Mound

Now the grasses are listening
all one way in the wind.
The horizon remains true,
though each year my roof is mumbled
lower by the snow and her daughters.

My bones, lying under it, see
by the turquoise and copper light
of a Pawnee chieftain. Each year
they glow a little brighter,
waiting for the great northern bear

who hunts over ice in winter,
who is the blindness of snow.
My bones swing like the silver needle
in the white trader's box. I listen:
the whole earth is rooted with lightning.

The bear, deep in frozen honey,
tears up the tundra for ants,
feasts on the solitude of graves.
Mound by mound he shambles southward,
his eye quick with arrows.

His claws shine for my treasures,
his black nose glistens.
Huge and shaggy he will lift me
in a muzzle stained red with berries,
and safe in his teeth I'll go home.

Draining a Mosquito Swamp

Our hipboots already hot
we waded through reeds
which beat against us with a soft popping sound,
stirring up islands of duckweed,
dull rainbows of mineral oil,
to cling to the wet rubber.
Dropping its whistle
the red-winged blackbird
flashed and vanished.

We lined up our shovel handles
ten steps apart
and began to dig underwater
by the feel of it, two shovels wide.
Reeds shook and toppled.
Lopped and naked roots bobbed
on the clouded water,
a yellow ghost expanding to both sides.

Each shovel rose,
careful as a brontosaurus
coming up for air,
water streaming from its jaws,
and deposited the mush
back in the water to one side.

In two hours we'd moved three hundred feet,
shoveling one behind the other,
our ditch marked by the draining mound

of mixed clay and roots we'd turned up.
Now we dug visible marshbottom
which came up belching.

By three, the water ran out.
The blackbird returned to scream
at us over red epaulets,
his reeds sun-baked now,
coated with yellow mud.
When the backhoe lumbered up
to deepen what we had begun,
we rested by its gleaming teeth,
joked, and crumpled cardboard cups,
steeped in the smell of drying vegetation.

By five, our ditch made a straight line
across that swamp, limiting
what would never survive definition,
what we had failed to imagine —
enormous, delicate, elusive —
the sweet mess of life.

Peonies

With names like Bleeding Heart and Duchess Slipper
they rose in great heaps on the wagon
as I crouched and cut the stems and crouched again
rhythmically to keep up with the tractor —
the black earth sweet and clinging to my shoes,
the Mexicans' speech about me like a necklace.

The smell of each one nodding against my cheek
as I stooped to pick it, the flush armfuls
of Michigan Beauties landing on the wagon
with a soft hush — cream, white, crimson,
and peach flecked with mauve or carmine —
such clumsy stooping to stand up in a heaven

of perfume and rapidly rising banks of flowers!
Soon my legs cramped and my shirt soaked through
from the wet petals. In rare five-minute breathers
the others smoked and laughed at the greenhorn
whose arms for the first time ached from lifting flowers,
who sat there stunned as from some shameful excess.

Soon the tractor started again and the load trembled.
We had less than an hour to get them to the cooler.
There girls in loose smocks stripped and packed them
in green paper to be flown out that evening
to weddings, banquets, and graduations,
where other girls, gathering in dresses,

would pause long enough for a picture
against the Virginia Dares, the Forever Yours,
the Carolina Mornings. While, back in the welcome cooler,
our wagon empty, our fingers sore from knives,
we'd stand about breathing the cold fragrance
crowding upon our brains like a dark music.

Vandals

A green edge of new leaves on the air,
the sun like straw, tricking among branches,
we took our Daisy Rangers, light and easy
in gabardine and the pad of last year's sneakers,
out to war upon the flowers, tulips
that hurt us with their color, standing in rows.

Motionless, as if waiting for instructions,
hearing some speech or music in the light, they stood,
soldiers we knew would come to no upright end
anyway. So from behind garages, by shrub borders,
we took quick aim and fired through their ranks,
watching them fold suddenly at the middle.

The nicked ones leaned slowly right or left,
drooping their gorgeous plumage like dragoons.
It was a perilous business: Squares and crescents,
set out last fall to vary red and yellow,
orange, purple, ivory, tiger-striped,
stood marshaling their colors within view
of neighbors washing cars and raking lawns.

One down, two — and then we'd run a block,
Crows in the high elms watched us, rascals
like ourselves, raucous at a distance.
Like them, we were suspected, never caught,
lurking in bulb catalogs with the ghost of crabgrass
to haunt the dreamers who patiently turn this earth —

like those other Vandals that cross our dreams
on shaggy ponies, painted blue-and-yellow,
drunkenly dividing the jewels, the women,
gorging themselves by the smoking village —
primitive haters of the garden that would grow
brilliant and still in the waste of the outlaw heart.

The Garden

Your head's a cabbage, a cauliflower, a rose.
Your legs, carrots dreaming in the ground.
Your hair, a patch of lettuce, of new corn
leaning with the wind, restless to run
over the horizon where roofs disappear.
Each day I give you water from a hose.

I come and take what I need from your body,
walking a path I have trampled across you
on loose boards that bang and flop.
Beets are blood I draw from you,
radishes, white and red, your lips and teeth,
and onions, your secret breath.

Not a word from you, not the slightest complaint,
no accusing look under the sky's blank stare.
I hate your silences, your perfect rhythms,
your language of consonants, of crickets singing —
no vowel squeezed from a human heart.
Yet you give and give. What am I to say?

I know what the apple tree is saying.
A tree is different. It yields one word
that stirs and ripens at the center.
It covers the grass with an emerald shadow
and bears a wisdom, upright and sincere.
It utters the day with a profusion of tongues

and fills the heart with a squeezing of apples.
But you are not like that at all:
Your fingers weave light on the horizon.
From a house, from a tree, a face peers out,
wondering what cargos crisscross the distance
as your night odors wreck on his doorstep
and the moon presses the length of her body against you.

Shopping Together

Cardboard stars crowd the shelves,
and moons marked off a penny,
as you glide, standing on the cart,

to a touch in any direction.
We shine in a dusk of eggplants,
sleepy with a perfume of apples,

wander forests of asparagus,
drift a green ocean
of lettuce, avocados, celery,

down an avalanche of oranges
to a wilderness of bananas —
an El Dorado of lavish aromas.

Still, beyond the parsley are berries
superfluous with juice
that break in our mouths like old sorrows,

and melons like a school of whales
shouldering a cool secret
over the edge of the world.

Last, as we count up our treasures
the register sings and the basket
bumps to the car with your laughter.

Once inside, all the way home,
bags leaning lovesick against us,
ice creams thawing in secret,
we feed each other plums and dark cherries.

The Moonseed

came floating down a beam
thin as a hair,
landing with a silvery
plink. But when I stooped to look —
lost between floorboards.

Mornings later a green feeler
poked through my mattress.
By afternoon
the whole mattress was
tilted off the springs a little,
invisibly rising and falling
to a plant's breath.

That night I dreamt a girl
green as a lima bean
unfolded from a leaf,
sighed in the creepers, her cool
presence waxing with the moon.

I held my breath
till morning, slid off,
locking the door behind me,
relieved the grass outside
was no higher than usual.

The next night, I slept
with my nose near the ceiling,
headlights skating over me from below.
Fearing I might be impressed

in the plaster forever,
I kept close to the edge.

About three the moonfruit ripened,
waking me with its light —
orange, blue, silver —
passing through all the phases,
stretching the shadow of my shoes
along the floor.

Perfect, white, it trembled.
I felt a stir beside me and the girl's
cool breasts brush my shoulder
as she floated to the floor,
took the fruit
and leaped out the window.

Darkness — groaning of boards — thrashing of stalks —
I dragged myself from the splintered bed
to the window. There,
over the restless field,
a green planet hung
nearly imbedded in the earth.

As it sank, my walls shuddered,
my roof waltzed off,
weeds broke through the floorboards.
I moved my blankets out to the field
and lay listening
to the sweet, all-night ticking of the grass.

Dandelions

for LP

My yard is solid yellow with dandelions.
They gather there for a convention,
arriving from all over, forming a carpet
too brilliant to look upon.
My white house blushes gold
as their fuzzy heads press against its clapboards.

Each of my neighbors snickers out his window
as the last squatters run, bright heads tossing,
to my place — leaving their lawns green and flat.
I open my window and breathe in the wine
of their fragrance, gold under me like Solomon.
All day they give the sun up to the sun.

All night pollen thickens around me.
I carefully gather and press it between pages
until I am empty and drained. The next morning
all have gone silver in a cloud, a mist
that you see a loved face through in a wet October.
I breathe out the window slowly upon them:

The white seeds shake, twinkle to be gone.
In a swirl they rise, weightless as gossamer,
obscuring windows, dissolving walls:
Houses, neighbors, blow into the sky,
lawns falling away like tiny emeralds,
as a thousand suns falter, vanish into light.

Like Butter

> *Up hill and down dale,*
> *Butter is made in every vale.*

for SJ

There is a light like butter.
Cut it and spread it over a hill,
a leaf, a finger.
Give your fingers away to the leaves:
See how white and perfect they become,
every knuckle like the Rocky Mountains,
every nail full as a rose.

If you let your hands hang down
and do not think about Abyssinia,
notice how your eyes run to the front,
how the sky steadies and the grass grows solid
underfoot, how what you are tingles in your fingers
and every pore opens to the sea.

Then the sad Sahara of the interior,
the black sands and infinite dry rock,
vanishes to a light that shows
between finger and thumb; the howling tribes
crack like drops from a frozen window
as Aldebaran winks in the drifting night.

Now put your hand to the sky: Its blue paint
smells yare and endless, and once again
a child,
you paint the wet black windows
on the leaf-red ferry.

Blackberries

As white as milk,
And not milk;
As green as grass,
And not grass;
As red as blood,
And not blood;
As black as soot,
And not soot.

—Old Riddle

Neither is this Thou,
Yet this also is Thou.

—Charles Williams

If there were true comfort in a glass of milk,
sheets, clouds, pillows, just as white,
if gardens always winked at the green
brim of morning and mind moved with the grass,
if flies contemplated the red
of roses without leaping for their blood,

I'd be content to feel my blood
map time and watch a mother's milk
run from the baby's mouth, or let the red
rose assassinate me and even the white
sleep of snow descend, for grass
would hold me always in its quaking green.

There are times I am webbed in the green
sliding leaves, times I think my blood
will burst the veins of grass
or the blue shadow from a glass of milk
on the table closes a white
wound within me, quieting its red

pulsing mouth. But, again, somewhere red
leaps from a gun and a green
light drains city faces and a white
terror of empty screens fills with blood,
collecting slowly as a mother's milk
under the understanding grass.

It is then I want the face slurred in that grass,
the outstretched hand pooling bottomless red,
offering it for drink — a second milk
in spring when the rolled stone gathers green
from the spilled blood
and an air like silk shatters to white.

Yet, what I want is white,
but not, can hold the mind like grass,
but through endless fields, and like blood
map who I am, but with a sharper red
than the rose's tooth, a greener green
than the cow swags for her summer milk.

Is even blacker than black: For, white, green,
and red, the earth is still unripe, though milk, grass
and the dear blood may dazzle beyond sight.

Rinsed with Gold, Endless, Walking the Fields

Let this day's air praise the Lord —
Rinsed with gold, endless, walking the fields,
Blue and bearing the clouds like censers,
Holding the sun like a single note
Running through all things, a *basso profundo*
Rousing the birds to an endless chorus.

Let the river throw itself down before him,
The rapids laugh and flash with his praise,
Let the lake tremble about its edges
And gather itself in one clear thought
To mirror the heavens and the reckless gulls
That swoop and rise on its glittering shores.

Let the lawn burn continually before him
A green flame, and the tree's shadow
Sweep over it like the baton of a conductor,
Let winds hug the housecorners and woodsmoke
Sweeten the world with her invisible dress,
Let the cricket wind his heartspring
And draw the night by like a child's toy.

Let the tree stand and thoughtfully consider
His presence as its leaves dip and row
The long sea of winds, as sun and moon
Unfurl and decline like contending flags.

Let blackbirds quick as knives praise the Lord,
Let the sparrow line the moon for her nest
And pick the early sun for her cherry,
Let her slide on the outgoing breath of evening,
Telling of raven and dove,
The quick flutters, homings to the green houses.

Let the worm climb a winding stair,
Let the mole offer no sad explanation
As he paddles aside the dark from his nose,
Let the dog tug on the leash of his bark,
The startled cat electrically hiss,
And the snake sign her name in the dust

In joy. For it is he who underlies
The rock from its liquid foundation,
The sharp contraries of the giddy atom,
The unimaginable curve of space,
Time pulling like a patient string,
And gravity, fiercest of natural loves.

At his laughter, splendor riddles the night,
Galaxies swarm from a secret hive,
Mountains lift their heads from the sea,
Continents split and crawl for aeons
To huddle again, and planets melt
In the last tantrum of a dying star.

At his least signal spring shifts
Its green patina over half the earth,

Deserts whisper themselves over cities,
Polar caps widen and wither like flowers.

In his stillness rock shifts, root probes,
The spider tenses her geometrical ego,
The larva dreams in the heart of the peachwood,
The child's pencil makes a shaky line,
The dog sighs and settles deeper,
And a smile takes hold like the feet of a bird.

Sit straight, let the air ride down your backbone,
Let your lungs unfold like a field of roses,
Your eyes hang the sun and moon between them,
Your hands weigh the sky in even balance,
Your tongue, swiftest of members, release a word
Spoken at conception to the sanctum of genes,
And each breath rise sinuous with praise.

Let your feet move to the rhythm of your pulse
(Your joints like pearls and rubies he has hidden),
And your hands float high on the tide of your feelings.
Now, shout from the stomach, hoarse with music,
Give gladness and joy back to the Lord,
Who, sly as a milkweed, takes root in your heart.

Robert Siegel

About the Author

Robert Siegel's first collection of poems, *The Beasts & the Elders,* appeared in 1973 from the University Press of New England. His first book of fiction, a pastoral romance entitled *Alpha Centauri,* will be published later this year by Cornerstone Books.

Among the awards he has received for his poems are *Poetry*'s Jacob Glatstein Prize, the *Prairie Schooner* Poetry Prize, the Chicago Poetry Prize, inclusion in *Best Poems of 1976*, an NEA Creative Writing Fellowship, an Ingram Merrill Foundation Award, the Cliff Dwellers' Arts Foundation Award, the *Transatlantic Review* Fellowship to Bread Loaf, residencies at Yaddo, and grants from Dartmouth and the University of Wisconsin.

He has degrees from Wheaton (Illinois), Johns Hopkins, and Harvard, and he has taught at Wheaton, Dartmouth, and Princeton. He is currently associate professor of English at the University of Wisconsin-Milwaukee. He lives with his wife Ann and three daughters in Whitefish Bay, Wisconsin.